THE HOW AND WHY WONDER® BOOK OF
SEA SHELLS

Written by DONALD F. LOW
Illustrated by CYNTHIA and ALVIN KOEHLER
Editorial Production: DONALD D. WOLF

Edited under the supervision of
Dr. Paul E. Blackwood, Washington, D.C.
Text and illustrations approved by
Oakes A. White, Brooklyn Children's Museum, Brooklyn, New York

PRICE/STERN/SLOAN
Publishers, Inc., Los Angeles
1983

W9-BRA-236

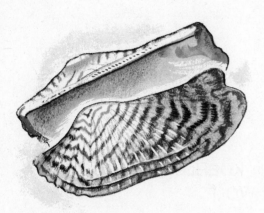

Introduction

If you see a snow-white angel wing or hold a cockle shell or examine a periwinkle, you will be fascinated with the beauty of sea shells and awed by the spectacular handiwork of nature. Yet these three shells are no more remarkable than thousands of others known to man. *The How and Why Wonder® Book of Sea Shells* describes the major groups of shell animals and tells about their habits. You will discover that there is an endless variety of shells. Some are small and delicate and beautifully colored. Some are huge and rough. Yet the shape, size and structure of each shell animal enables it to live its own particular style of life.

Do you know what the *Juno's volute* and the *precious wentletrap* look like? These are rare shells and they are collector's dreams. But more common shells are fun to collect, too, except perhaps some huge ones that are almost too heavy to lift. One must be able to observe carefully to classify carefully. Ability to observe is important to scientists. Studying the characteristics of shells to organize them into collections will help young people develop this ability.

The How and Why Wonder® Book of Sea Shells is just the book for beginning shell collectors. It is a publication which children and parents can enjoy together at home, and one which teachers and children can use with profit at school.

Paul E. Blackwood

Dr. Blackwood is a professional employee in the U. S. Office of Education. This book was edited by him in his private capacity and no official support or endorsement by the Office of Education is intended or should be inferred.

Copyright© 1961 by Price/Stern/Sloan Publishers, Inc.
Published by Price/Stern/Sloan Publishers, Inc.
410 North La Cienega Boulevard, Los Angeles, California 90048

Printed in the United States of America. All rights reserved. No part of this publication may be reproduced, stored in a retrieval system, or transmitted, in any form or by any means, electronic, mechanical, photocopying, recording, or otherwise, without the prior written permission of the publishers.

ISBN: 0-8431-4275-8

Library Congress Catalog Card Number 61-1762

How and Why Wonder® Books is a trademark of Price/Stern/Sloan Publishers, Inc.

Contents

LITTLE GREEN RAZOR CLAM

LENTIL ASTARTE

EARED ARK

The shoreline is an excellent place to find shell specimens, especially at low tide.

CARPENTER'S TELLIN

COMMON PERIWINKLE

ATLANTIC OYSTER DRILL

CALIFORNIA PINK SCALLOP

SUNRISE TELLIN

JINGLE SHELLS

WAVED ASTARTES

BLUE MUSSELS

FALSE ANGEL WING

ROUGH-SIDED LITTLENECK

HOOKED MUSSEL

ATLANTIC
DEEP-SEA SCALLOP

THORNY SCALLOP

ATLANTIC SURF CLAM

SOFT-SHELL CLAM

PISMO CLAM

Mollusks

Why do mollusks need shells?

Have you ever taken a walk along the beach to collect shells? Probably most of the shells you found were once the homes of living animals called mollusks, a name which comes from the Latin word *mollis,* meaning "soft." This is a true description of mollusks' bodies, which have no bones. Soft bodies need support, such as bony skeletons give to many kinds of animals. In fact, a mollusk's hard shell serves as its skeleton —a skeleton on the outside of its body!

Mollusks are sought as food not only by man, but by many animals that live in the water and on land. Hard shells, however, protect mollusks from many of their enemies.

ATLANTIC BAY SCALLOP

TREE OYSTER

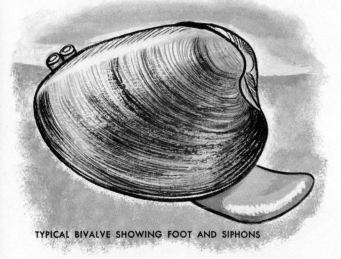

TYPICAL BIVALVE SHOWING FOOT AND SIPHONS

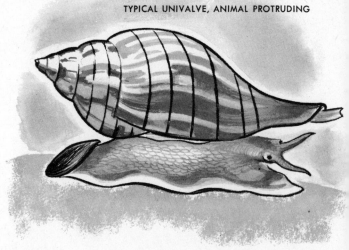

There are thousands of species of mollusks. Indeed, the

Where do mollusks live? mollusk division, or phylum, popularly called shellfish, makes up one of the largest groups in the animal kingdom. Although a few kinds of mollusks live on land, and a larger number in fresh-water streams and lakes, the largest number live in the ocean.

Those that live at the shoreline, like oysters and mussels, must adapt themselves to being "sea animals" at high tide when the water covers them, and "land animals" at low tide when the water recedes. At low tide, their shells provide them with protection from the sun which would otherwise dry out their soft, unprotected bodies.

The mollusks are not only one of the largest groups of animals, they are also one of the oldest. Fossil remains indicate that they have been common in the seas for more than a half-billion years.

There is great variety among mollusks.

How big are mollusks? Some are so small as to be scarcely visible to the unaided eye.

Some, such as the giant squid, are as much as 50 feet long. The shells of many mollusks are beautifully colored and exquisitely shaped. Many are delicately carved. There are red, orange, yellow, brown, pink, lavender and rainbow-hued shells. Some resemble basket weaving and others are marked with spots and stripes in an almost endless variety of designs.

The Five Classes of Mollusks

To make it easier to study the many thousands of different species of mollusks, scientists have grouped them into five major classes: bivalves, univalves, chitons, tusk shells, and cephalopods.

Bivalves are the two-shelled mollusks,

What are bivalves? including clams, oysters and mussels. Their shells are joined by a hinge of tough tendon and are held together by one or two powerful muscles. These

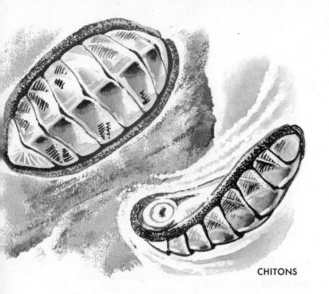

CHITONS

TUSK, ANIMAL PROTRUDING

TYPICAL CEPHALOPOD

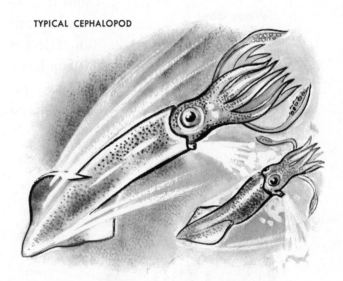

mollusks are also called *pelecypods,* a word meaning "hatchet-footed" which refers to the shape of their single "foot."

Univalves are the one-shelled mollusks,

What are univalves?

including snails, abalones, whelks and conchs. They are also called *gastropods,* a word meaning "stomach-footed." As other animals crawl about on their stomachs, the gastropod uses its large muscular "foot," which extends from its shell, for the same purpose.

Chitons are the most primitive of the

What are chitons?

mollusks — the ones that appeared first in the history of living things. The mollusks in this class all have one thing in common: a shell made up of eight separate and overlapping plates. The plates are bound together by a tough, leathery girdle made of cartilage. If the girdle is removed, the plates fall apart.

Tusk shells, or *tooth shells* are the

What are tusk shells?

smallest class of mollusks. Their shells are in the form of tubes, much like elephant tusks, but much smaller, of course.

Cephalopods, which means "head-

What are cephalopods?

footed," are mollusks that include squids, cuttlefish and octopuses. They were given this name because they have a number of arms, or feet, that extend from their heads. Unlike the other mollusks, most cephalopods have no surrounding shells, but a short, narrow blade within the body.

7

Bivalves

The bivalves are by far the largest of the five classes of mollusks. Because of their value as food, they form the most important class for man, and are the chief sources of pearls and mother-of-pearl. They are found in all parts of the world—some in fresh-water streams and lakes, but most of them in tidepools and the seas and oceans.

If you pry open the shells of a bivalve,

What does the inside of a bivalve look like?

you will find it difficult to make out head or tail. There is no distinct head and the organs are arranged in an unusual way, compared with most animals. The mouth is near

in the mud or sandy bottom of the sea. Then, as it draws the foot back into the shell, the bivalve pulls itself forward.

Just at the other end of the foot is a large

How do bivalves breathe and eat?

muscular pair of tubes called *siphons*. The tube can be poked far out of the shell and was mistaken by some people for the neck of the bivalve. From this error, the names "littleneck" and "longneck" clam resulted. Water is drawn into one of the siphons, bringing with it oxygen and tiny bits of food. This water then picks up waste products and is expelled

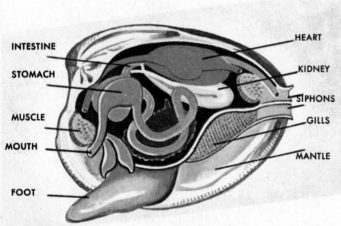

INTESTINE
STOMACH
MUSCLE
MOUTH
FOOT
HEART
KIDNEY
SIPHONS
GILLS
MANTLE

The internal organs of a bivalve

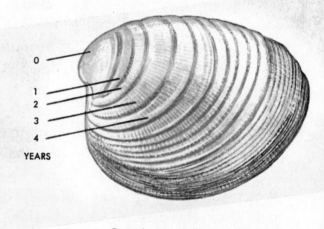

0
1
2
3
4
YEARS

Growth-rings indicate shell's age.

the foot, the stomach lies higher than the mouth and the food tube passes through the heart. Most bivalves move by means of the thick, muscular foot that is pushed out of the bottom of the open shell. The animal anchors its foot

from the shell through the other siphon. When bivalves are buried in mud, they can extend the siphon tubes above the surface of the mud and get food and oxygen. The oxygen that is dissolved in the water is taken up by the bivalve's gills, and carbon dioxide is given off the same way.

Lining the shell is a membrane called the *mantle*, which uses minerals that are in the water to form a three-layer shell around the soft body of the bivalve. The outer layer is thin and made of a hornlike material; the middle one is limy, thick and hard; the inner layer of some bivalve shells is composed of the material called *mother-of-pearl*.

What does the mantle do?

It is this material that gives the inside

The shells of bivalves grow with their occupants. Some bivalves increase their size at a faster rate in the warm months than in the cold months, and their shells indicate annual growth-rings, much like the growth-rings of trees. Just as you can tell the age of a tree by counting the number of its rings, you can also tell the age of certain bivalves by counting the growth rings on their shells.

How can you tell the age of a bivalve?

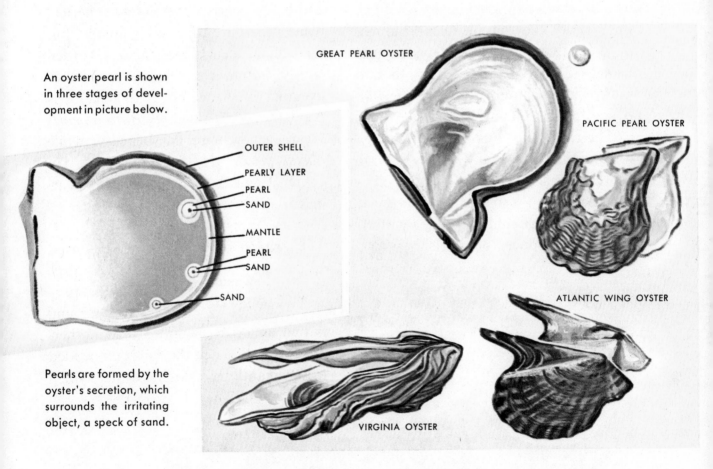

An oyster pearl is shown in three stages of development in picture below.

OUTER SHELL
PEARLY LAYER
PEARL
SAND
MANTLE
PEARL
SAND
SAND

GREAT PEARL OYSTER

PACIFIC PEARL OYSTER

ATLANTIC WING OYSTER

VIRGINIA OYSTER

Pearls are formed by the oyster's secretion, which surrounds the irritating object, a speck of sand.

of oysters, mussels and many other shells a pearly iridescence. The mantle secretes the shell and also acts as an organ of sense, for imbedded in its margin are nerve cells which are sensitive to light and touch.

Oysters

The most valuable of the bivalves are *oysters*, which are common in the shallow and warmer waters of all oceans. Oysters have irregular shells, and in most species the two halves are unequal in size — the upper valve is usually smaller than the lower one.

How many eggs can a female oyster lay?
A female oyster produces between five and fifty million eggs a year, but few of them mature. Within a day after an egg is fertilized, the shell begins to form. For a few days after oysters hatch from their eggs, they swim about freely. Then they attach themselves to a rock or some other submerged object upon which they usually spend the rest of their lives. Full-grown oysters are usually 2 to 10 inches in length and many kinds, among them the *Virginia oyster,* are excellent food.

The *great pearl oyster,* found in Ceylon and the Persian Gulf, grows as large as 12 inches. The inside of its shell is covered with a beautiful layer of mother-of-pearl, and the oyster is itself a famous producer of pearls.

How do oysters form pearls?
If a foreign object, usually a small parasite, but perhaps a sharp grain of sand, finds its way into the mantle of an oyster, it causes an irritation. In order to soothe this irritation, the oyster secretes its mother-of-pearl-forming substance around the object. Gradually, layer by layer, a pearl is formed.

Most pearls are white, faintly yellowish or bluish, but there are also pink, purple, blue, green, yellow, red, brown and black pearls. Completely spherical white pearls are the most valuable, but fine black pearls are also regarded highly. *Baroque,* or *Oriental,* pearls are irregular in shape, but if their color is good, they are in demand. *Button pearls* are those that are flat beneath, while *blister pearls* are those that have become attached to the mother-of-pearl of the shell.

How can man make pearls?
The growth of pearls may be started artificially. A piece is cut from the mantle of an oyster and is tied as a sac around a tiny mother-of-pearl ball. Then the sac is embedded in the mantle of another oyster which

OYSTER EGGS

SWIMMING STAGE

6 MONTHS OLD

1 YEAR OLD

Development of an oyster, and adult *Eastern oyster* with its young attached to the shell.

Florida tree oysters hang on the roots of mangrove and other trees which grow above the ground in swampland.

is returned to the water. After three or four years, a fine pearl is formed. Pearls made in this manner are called *cultured* pearls, or *Mikomoto* pearls after the name of the Japanese discoverer of the process. Pearls are also formed in the shells of both salt- and fresh-water mussels.

The *winged tree oyster,* a native of the Florida coast, has greatly compressed shells — one valve is flat and the other is only slightly raised. The surface of each valve is sometimes smooth, sometimes scaly, and the color purplish, black or brown. The inside of the shell has a pearly layer that does not extend to the edges. This animal is called a tree oyster because it lives in large colonies attached to the roots of mangrove and other trees in the Florida swamps. The roots of these trees grow above ground, and may be alternately covered and uncovered by the tide. Thus, this oyster actually lives in trees.

Which oysters live in trees?

Mussels

The *mussel* family of bivalves includes more than a dozen species, among which the *blue mussel* is the most common. When fully grown it is about 3 inches long. This mussel is in-

Blue mussels attach themselves to rocks and pilings.

teresting because of the way it attaches itself to rocks and pier pilings in order to keep from being smothered by the sediment at the bottom of the water.

The young blue mussel alternately touches and withdraws its foot from a rock several times, an action **How do mussels fight off the ocean waves?** which leaves a sticky thread attached both to the rock and to the mussel's shell. As the threads are made, a special gland in the mussel's body bathes them in a secretion that makes them hard and tough enough to resist the pounding force of most ocean waves. When, rarely, a mussel changes its place of anchorage, it breaks the threads, called a *byssus,* one by one. Mussels are edible, and the European species are considered delicacies.

Clams

A small group of edible bivalves are the *clams,* one of whose species, the *hard-shell clam,* is found along the eastern coast of the United States from Maine to Florida. It is also called *cherrystone, littleneck* or *round clam,* while the Indians called it the *quahog,* a name by which it is still known in New England. When fully grown it has a shell 5 or 6 inches in length, which is grayish white in color. The inside of the shell is white, with a purple border at the edges.

Like *Northern quahogs,* clams were used for wampum.

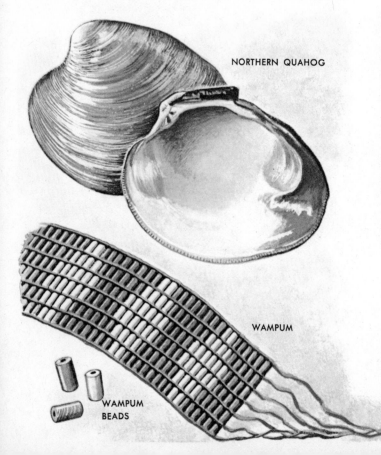

NORTHERN QUAHOG

WAMPUM

WAMPUM BEADS

The quahog was not only a favorite food of the Indians, but was also used by them as **Which shell was used as money?** money. From the shell, they carved and ground beads and disks called *wampum.* These were pierced in the center

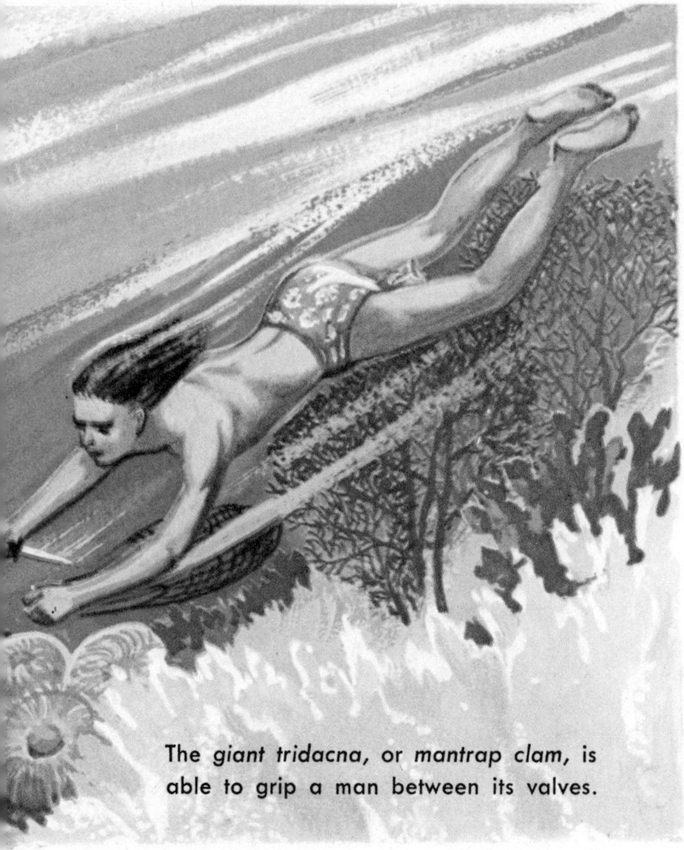

The *giant tridacna, or mantrap clam,* is able to grip a man between its valves.

and strung together or woven into belts. The strings of wampum served as money, the belts as tokens to bind treaties. One of the most famous treaty wampums was the belt given to William Penn to record a land treaty with the Indians in Pennsylvania. Another use for wampum was the keeping of important records by sewing the beads in special patterns on deerskin belts.

Which shell can trap a man?

Although many bivalves are caught by man for their value as food, there is one bivalve, however, that is able to catch a man — not to eat him, however. This giant mollusk is the *tridacna,* also known as the *mantrap clam*. It lives in the tropical waters of the South Pacific, and if you start a shell collection, it is not likely that you will count this clam among your collection. The animal alone weighs between 25 and 30 pounds, and the shells as much as 600 pounds. The muscles that move the two valves are so strong that a man caught between the powerful shells would not be able to free himself. Despite vivid accounts in books of fiction, however, there is no actual record of any man having been caught in the grip of a tridacna.

The natives of the South Pacific islands use the shell as a source of material for tools, and the meat is usually enough for a community feast. Many years ago, at the celebrations surrounding the birth of a native chieftain's son, the child was first bathed in the sea and then in a sacred tridacna shell.

How big is the tiny gem?

The shell of the tiny *gem clam,* when fully grown, is no more than 1/5 of an inch long. It is broadly triangular in shape and has a

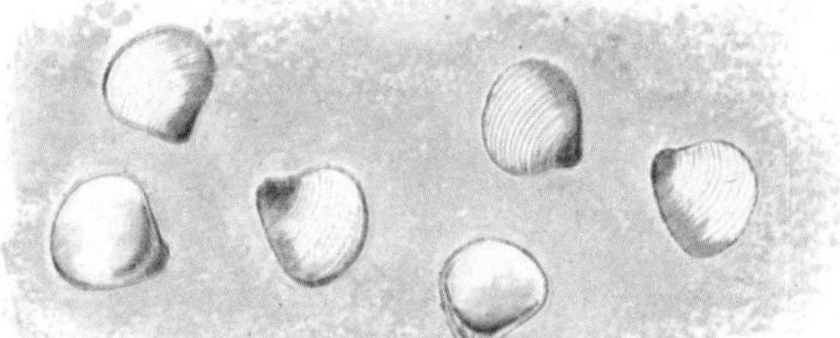

The tiny *gem clam* is one of the smallest bivalves.

shining surface marked with concentric lines. Because of its color, pale lavender outside and shaded white to purplish on the inside, it is often called the *amethyst gem clam*. These bivalves, which are found in quantity on the sandy shores of the Atlantic Coast, were once believed to be the young of quahogs, which they resemble.

Tellins

One of the attractions that makes col-

Which are the most colorful shells?

lecting shells so interesting is the color of the specimens. There is not a color of the rainbow or a color combination that is not found in some shell, but for

The *rose petal tellin* is common to the South Atlantic.

their delicate hues and shades, the bivalves of the *tellin* family are considered to be the nobility of the varicolored shells. Tellins are natives of all seas, and the family has more than a hundred species. All are highly polished, and their colors range from the rosy pink of the *rose petal tellin*, the yellowish white of the *rising sun tellin*, the pure white of the *linen tellin*, to the dark purple of the *carpenter's tellin*.

Scallops

Oysters attach themselves to some object, mussels bind themselves to rocks or piling, clams live dug into the sand. In short, most adult bivalves do not move about very much. But the family of *scallops*, or *pectens*, are quite active swimmers. Unlike the young of mussels

and oysters, which are free-swimming, the young of scallops are attached by a byssus to a stationary object, and it is the adults which are free-swimming.

One might say that adult scallops jet-

How do scallops move?

propel themselves through the water. The two valves of the scallop are usually unequal in size, the lower one convex, the upper one flat or even concave. The shell surfaces of most species in this family are ribbed and the edges are curved. The animal moves by opening and closing its two shells quickly and strongly, thereby forcing out water from between the valves. The force of the water shooting out drives the animal in the opposite direction. The favored edible part, incidentally, is the powerful muscle that snaps the valves shut.

Scallops differ from other bivalves in another way. They have a row of tiny eyes—each complete with cornea, lens and optic nerve — located on the edge of the mantle. Some species have thirty or more eyes.

The most common scallop of the At-

How big are they?

lantic Coast is the *bay scallop*. It is about 3 inches in length, and may be white, brown, gray or yellow. Similar in color, but larger, is the *San Diego scallop*. It is between 5 and 8 inches long and lives in deep waters. The *thorny scallop* is only about 1 inch long and may be bright scarlet, purple, white, brown or mottled in color. Most scallops prefer shallow water and are more common along the Atlantic than

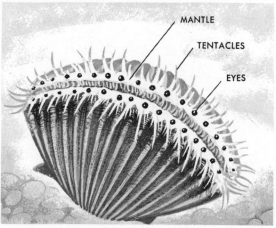

Scallops swimming (left); scallop showing tentacles, mantle and eyes (below).

the Pacific shores. They vary in size from 1 to 8 inches. Scallops are usually the mainstay of a shell collection because of their many shapes and beautiful colors, which vary from pink and rose to yellow and brown.

Scallops have frequently appealed to painters and architects. In the Middle Ages, many crusaders who fought in the Holy Land returned home wearing the *St. James scallop* as a badge of honor. These shells later appeared on many coats of arms in Europe as a sign that members of the family had fought in the Crusades.

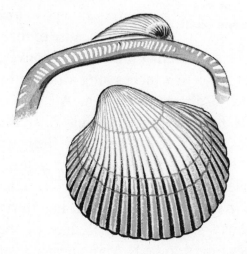

Arks

Ark shells are heavy, stiff and ribbed. The animals that live in them have no siphons, and they are more common along the Atlantic than the Pacific Coast. One of the most easily found is the *turkey wing,* or *Noah's ark shell,* which is between 2 and 3 inches long. It is striped with brown on the outside, and is light lavender on the inside.

Most mollusks have colorless or light pink blood, but there **Do they have red blood?** is one species, the *blood ark,* that has red blood. It lives on the shallow, sandy bottom of the sea, has a shell with thirty-five prominent ribs and a dark brown hairy coating.

The *blood ark* is the only mollusk that has red blood. The hinge line of an ark shell is pictured in detail.

15

Butterfly Shells

Butterfly shells are bivalves which are also called *coquina* and *wedge shells*. They are very small — less than 1 inch in length — and are found in abundance at the shorelines of the Atlantic, Pacific and Gulf coasts.

Can they fly?

BUTTERFLY SHELLS

The butterfly shell cannot fly — no shellfish can. Its common name is derived from the fact that when the animal dies, the valves, which remain hinged, spread open like a butterfly's wings. These shells are also colored like the wings of some butterflies. They range from white, yellow, and lavender over pale blue, to deep purple. Some are striped and others have a distinct plaid pattern.

Pen Shells

The *sea pens*, or *pen shells,* are a family of bivalves that got their name from their appearance. They have wedge-shaped shells, 4 inches to 1 foot long, that look much like old-fashioned quill pens. Pens prefer the warm, deep waters where they attach themselves, buried in the sand, to pebbles and rocks. One of the most common species is the *stiff sea pen* that has an olive brown shell decorated with

Can you write with a sea pen?

about fifteen elevated ribs. It is found along the eastern seaboard from North Carolina to the coast of South America. The byssus of this bivalve is made of olive-golden threads that are said to have been gathered in Italy, centuries ago, and woven into caps and gloves. Another fairly common species is the *saw-toothed pen* whose shell is brownish black with closely-set ribs.

Although you can't write with a sea pen, you can eat the large muscle of this shellfish.

Cockle Shells

You may know the old song about Molly Malone going through the streets of Dublin selling "Cockles and mussels,/Alive, alive O!" Or you probably still remember the famous nursery rhyme: "Mary, Mary, quite contrary,/How does your garden grow?/With silver bells and cockle shells,/And pretty maids all in a row."

Cockle shells, about which Molly and Mary sing, or *heart shells* as they are called because of their shape, are another family of bivalves. They are 1 to 7 inches long and can be found in almost every sea. All cockle shells have strong radiating ribs, the valves are of equal size, and they are colored red, orange, brown, yellow, purple or white. The *giant Atlantic cockle* is 3 or 4 inches long, has thirty to thirty-six ribs and the edges of the valves are toothed. Many species of cockles are edible.

What are cockle shells?

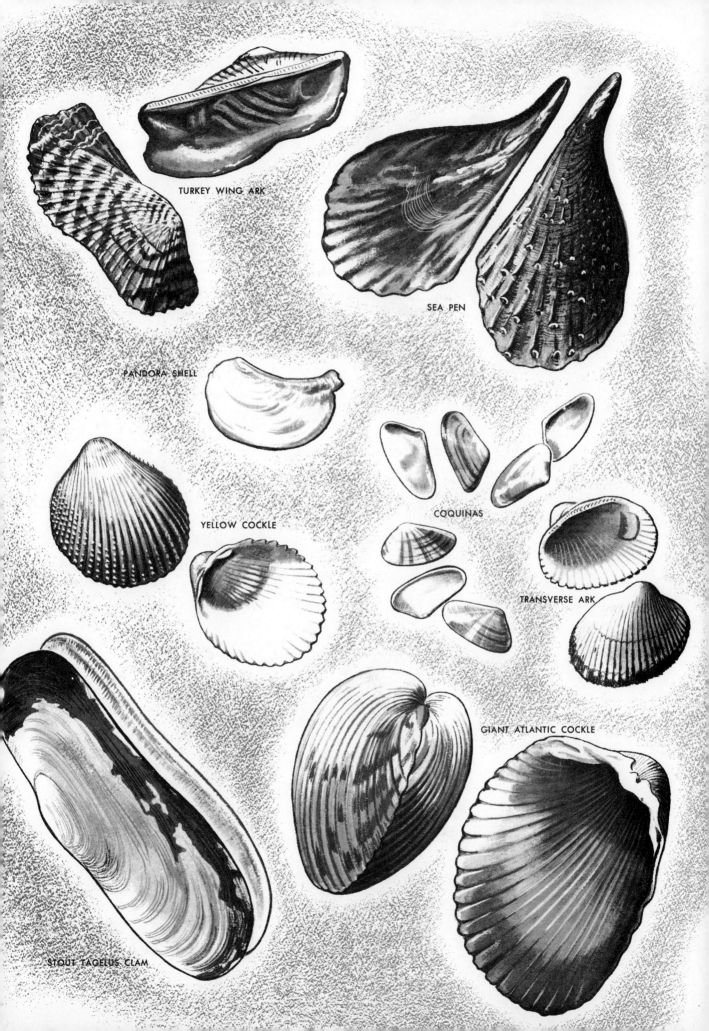

TURKEY WING ARK

SEA PEN

PANDORA SHELL

YELLOW COCKLE

COQUINAS

TRANSVERSE ARK

GIANT ATLANTIC COCKLE

STOUT TAGELUS CLAM

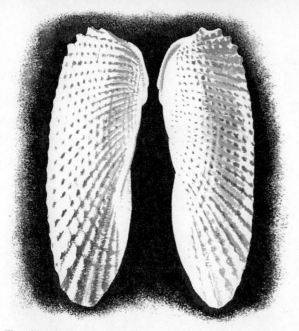

The thin-shelled *angel wing* is often pinkish in color.

if this doesn't make it difficult enough for the collector to find, the angel wing's shell is very fragile, so that it is hard to dig it out of the sand without breaking.

Despite their fragile shells, some species can bore holes in solid rock. One end of the shell is quite rough, and by turning and twisting it against a rock, the shellfish can make a hole large enough to hold itself. Angel wings occur from Cape Cod to the West Indies, and are also known as *piddocks*.

Angel Wings

The *angel wing* is extremely well named. It is a snowy-white brittle shell, 6 or 7 inches long, with radiating ribs about one-half inch apart — thus, it resembles an angel's wing. This bivalve burrows as deep as one foot beneath the sand, and

How did it get its name?

Shipworm

Butterfly shells are not butterflies, sea pens are not pens, and nor, for that matter, is a *shipworm* actually a worm, but a bivalve with a globular shell no larger than ¼-inch. The shell is at one end of a 6-inch tube which covers the animal.

Are there any harmful bivalves?

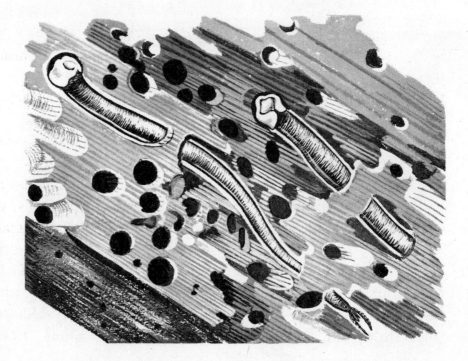

Shipworms, of which there are more than a dozen species, are sea scavengers.

The shipworm enters the wood of ships while it is still young and there it matures, digging a cylindrical, twisting burrow. Infested timber looks like a honeycomb and eventually disintegrates. This harmful little mollusk, whose control by the shipping industry is still a major problem, is also a welcome scavenger, because it rids harbors and shipping lanes of floating and sunken timber. The shipworm is also called the *teredo.*

Univalves

The univalves ("one-shelled"), or *gastropods* ("stomach-footed"), are the second main class of mollusks. They are less important commercially than the bivalves, but are more interesting to the collector because of their color and bizarre forms. As the name suggests, the animal has only one shell which it carries about like a hump on its back. Some univalves, such as the *garden slug,* have no shell at all, but because of their physical characteristics, are still classified as gastropods.

How do the univalves differ from the bivalves?

The foot of the univalve, like that of the bivalve, is a strong muscle. In case of danger, it withdraws the foot—and all other exposed parts of the body—into its shell, and closes the opening with a leather-like trap door called an *operculum.*

The opening of a univalve's shell is called the *mouth,* and the edges of the mouth are the *lips,* whose form and color varies with the species. In some shells the lip is thin and narrow, in others it is thick and wide. Some tropical univalves have spines sticking out from the lips in all directions, making the shell look like a huge spider.

Unlike the bivalves, the univalves have a distinct head with eyes and organs of feeling, smell and taste, all of which are contained in two pairs of tentacles on the head. The shorter pair at the front of the head is for feeling, smell and taste, and the longer pair farther back on the head contains the eyes at the tips.

On the head, too, is a distinct mouth with a tongue-like organ called the *radula,* which has many rows of spine-like teeth. Thus, the animal can tear or cut its food, scrape small plants from stones and even drill through the shells of other mollusks.

The shells of univalves are more or less spiral in shape, though the body of the animal is not similarly coiled.

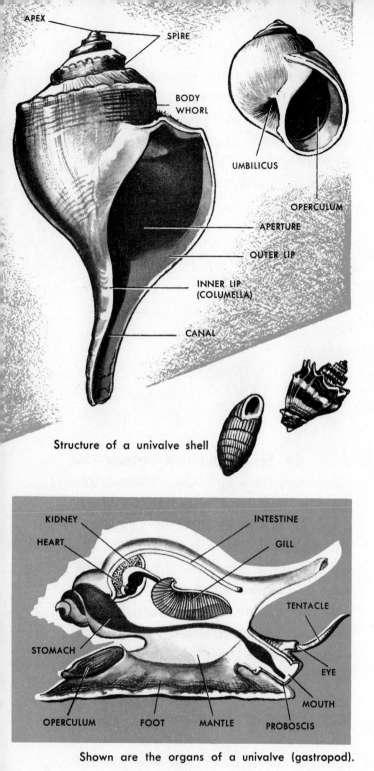

APEX
SPIRE
BODY WHORL
UMBILICUS
OPERCULUM
APERTURE
OUTER LIP
INNER LIP (COLUMELLA)
CANAL

Structure of a univalve shell

KIDNEY
HEART
INTESTINE
GILL
TENTACLE
STOMACH
EYE
MOUTH
OPERCULUM
FOOT
MANTLE
PROBOSCIS

Shown are the organs of a univalve (gastropod).

ESOPHAGUS
MOUTH
MUSCLE
RADULA (TONGUE)

The mouth part of a univalve is shown enlarged.

The foot, tentacles and eyes protrude from univalve.

How do they breathe? Otherwise, the body organs and their arrangement are similar to that of bivalves, modified, of course, to fit the coiled shell. Like bivalves, they breathe through gills. But univalves that live on land have no gills. They have air sacs that act as lungs, allowing the animal to obtain oxygen directly from the air. The land species are called *snails*. As a result, many water species are called *sea snails*.

Most gastropods lay eggs in the form of gelatin-like masses. Some look like strings, some like strands of wampum, and some are capsules that resemble oats and corn.

How is the univalve shell built? Just as in the bivalves, the univalve shell is secreted by a mantle that uses limy mineral dissolved in the water. As the shell becomes too small for the growing animal, it builds a new and larger section attached to the original. In this way the shell grows in the form of a coil wound about a central core, or *columella*. This

20

column is the main support of the shell and in some species is beautifully developed. In order to see the columella, however, you must perform the difficult task of cutting through the very hard shell.

When a gastropod crawls forward, the point of the shell always faces in the opposite direction. In most cases, the spiral whorls on the outside of the shell twist to the right. Among some species, the shell spirals twist to the left. These are called left-handed shells. In extremely rare cases, a normally right-handed shell is left-handed.

Cowries

The *cowry* family includes a large group of highly

Where were they used as money?

polished and brightly colored shells with "teeth" on both lips. These shells were, until not long ago, used as money in Africa and the South Pacific and were perhaps the first type of money ever used by man. Most cowries are tropical species and only a very few occur in the warmer waters of the North American coastline.

The *measled cowry* is found in the shallow waters of the eastern seaboard from North Carolina on southward. It is 4 inches long and colored purplish brown with round whitish spots. The *little yellow cowry* is no more than 1 inch long when fully grown. This yellowish-white shell, spotted with yellow, is found along pebbled beaches from Florida on southward.

Like other univalves, the cowry has a spiral shell. How-

Why is the cowry glossy outside as well as inside?

ever, the spiral structure can be seen only when the animal is young, for as it grows, the lime deposits fill in the twists. In grown-up cowries, all trace of the spiral is lost. Its mantle grows out of the shell's mouth and covers both sides of the valves in two lobes that meet at the back of the shell. The result is that the cowry shell is as smooth on the outside as on the inside.

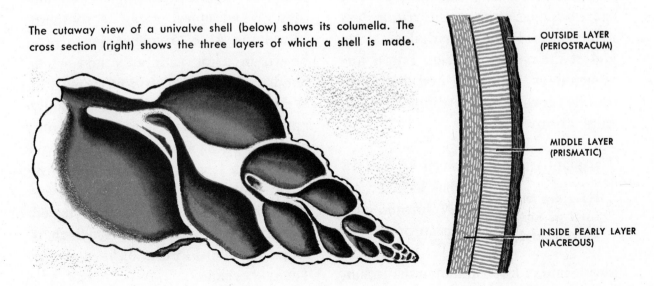

The cutaway view of a univalve shell (below) shows its columella. The cross section (right) shows the three layers of which a shell is made.

OUTSIDE LAYER (PERIOSTRACUM)

MIDDLE LAYER (PRISMATIC)

INSIDE PEARLY LAYER (NACREOUS)

Here are two views of the *measled cowry*.

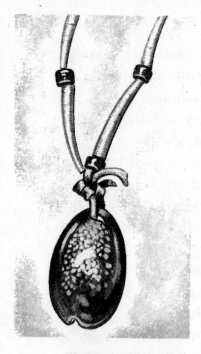
The North American Indians fashioned ornamental strings of cowry shells for decoration.

The *chestnut cowry* bears a resemblance to the nut, its namesake.

French fur trappers introduced cowry shells to the North American Indians who became so fond of them that strings of cowries were worn as signs of wealth, and later were buried with the wearer as his most prized possession.

Tritons

The *triton* family, with thousands of species including the *giant triton*, was named after Triton, a mythological sea god of the ancient Greeks. Triton was depicted as half man and half fish, usually blowing on his trumpet shell to calm stormy seas.

The giant triton is between 16 and 18 inches long, gracefully formed and multicolored with shades of brown, purple and red. It is found in the Indian

How are tritons used as musical instruments?

Ocean and the seas near Japan and the Philippines. Natives make trumpets from empty tritons by cutting a hole in the spire — the tapering part between the body and point of the shell. These instruments produce a tone not unlike a foghorn. Some South Sea Islanders use the empty shells as water containers.

Some species of the triton family are found in waters bordering the United States. The *hairy triton* of southern Florida is 4 to 6 inches long, pale brown in color with gray and white bands. The *angular triton,* usually a West Indian shell, though occasionally appearing in southern Florida, is one of the larger species and averages 7 to 8 inches in length. It is pale yellowish brown with darker bands. The pale yellow *ribbed triton* is a strong, rugged univalve, 3 to 4 inches long, which is found in the Florida Keys and the Texas shoreline.

Murex Shells

Closely related to the tritons are the many species of *murex shells* which vary greatly in color and size. The shell of the murex, like the triton's, is thick and solid, but the lips are rounder and smaller. This spiny univalve prefers moderately deep water, but the shells, which range in color from white upon yellow, orange, and pink to tan and light brown, are often washed up on the beaches. The most colorful murex species are found in tropical waters.

The ancient Phoenicians and other Mediterranean peoples made a purplish dye from a gland

How does the murex produce "dye" and "odors"?

in the mantle of the murex. This color, a dull crimson or magenta, was the "royal purple" of ancient times and was greatly valued for dyeing the robes of kings and nobles. Another gland in the murex produces a colored fluid that has the faint odor of garlic, which the animal ejects when it is in danger. The smell probably makes the murex distasteful to its enemies, and the colored fluid helps to conceal its retreat.

The *apple murex*, a heavy, rough shell of about 3 inches, is colored dark brown to yellow and tinged with rose. It is found in Atlantic waters from North Carolina to Florida. The brownish-black *lace murex* is an eagerly-sought collector's item because of its beautifully sculptured shell of rounded

The *ribbed triton* is found along the coasts of Florida and Texas. The *giant triton*, found in the Far East and South Seas, makes a good trumpet.

GIANT TRITON

RIBBED TRITON

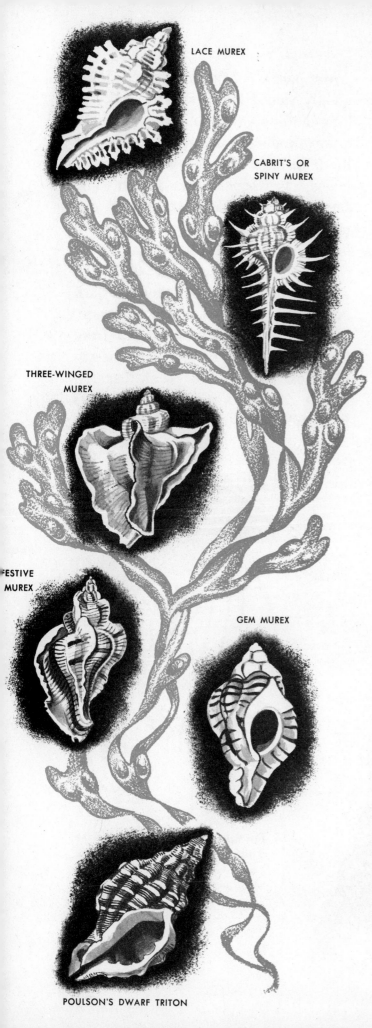

LACE MUREX

CABRIT'S OR SPINY MUREX

THREE-WINGED MUREX

FESTIVE MUREX

GEM MUREX

POULSON'S DWARF TRITON

spiraling cords crossed by riblike thickenings. This shell can be found in waters from North Carolina to South America, and is 1 to 2 inches long. The inside of the valve and the lips are a delicate pink when the animal is full-grown. In the young, the outside of the shell is a pale grayish pink.

A rare and valuable member of the family is the *spiny murex,* or *Cabrit's murex,* which is found in the waters of southern Florida, Texas and the West Indies. It is 3 inches long and pale pink in color. The sturdy shell has an elongated narrow canal that looks like a long spike, and its whorls are decorated with spines of various lengths. Wider than most other murex shells is the *Western three-winged murex,* which gets its name from the winglike structure of the shell. The valve, light or dark brown, is 2 or 3 inches long and sometimes has white spiral bands.

Drills and Dogwinkles

All members of the triton and murex families are *car-*

Why do fishermen dislike drills and dogwinkles?

nivorous, which means that they are flesh-eaters. The *oyster drills* and *dogwinkles,* two species of univalve closely related to the triton and murex, have developed a special taste for oysters on which they feed exclusively, causing a yearly damage of thousands of dollars to oyster beds. They use their rasplike tongue to drill a hole in the oyster's shell into which they insert a tube to suck out most of the oyster.

Oyster drills and dogwinkles, which look like miniature murex shells, vary in size from ½ to 3 inches. Some important species are the *Atlantic* and the *Tampa* oyster drills; the *file, Atlantic* and *emarginate* dogwinkles. These univalves live on rocks in shallow water or tide pools and are common in temperate waters around the world. The ancient Romans obtained a purple dye from their glands.

Carrier Shells

A univalve with the very strange habit of starting a collection of shells early in its life is the *carrier shell*. It begins, when very young, to fasten small bits of coral, small pebbles or little bivalve shells to the upper surface of its own shell. As the carrier grows it adds more and larger pieces until, when fully grown, the animal has enveloped its shell with a spiral of foreign material. The purpose of all this collecting is camouflage. Enemies of the carrier,

Who was the first shell collector?

looking at it from above, see only what appears to be a pile of debris.

It is not simply a jest that they were the first collectors. Fossil carrier shells have been found in rocks that geologists consider to be one hundred million years old. It is also not too difficult to understand why this shell, which is about 2 inches in diameter and yellowish brown in color, is called a "carrier."

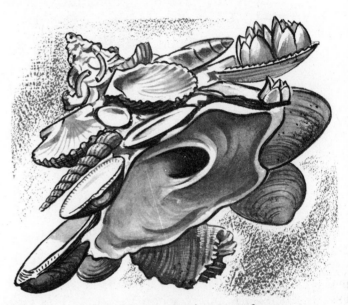

The carrier shell avoids enemies by camouflage.

ATLANTIC
OYSTER DRILL

FILE
DOGWINKLE

The oyster drill bores through the shell of an oyster for its dinner.

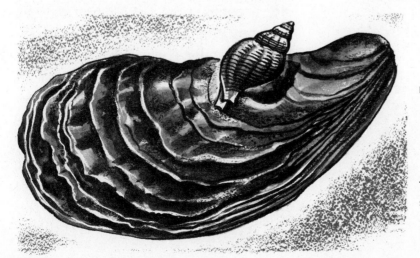

Violet Shell

The *violet shell*, or *purple snail*, is two-toned in color — violet above and purple below. Its delicate, fragile, 1½-inch shell has a thin, sharp outer lip. Two facts make the violet shell different from most other univalves. First, it does not have an operculum — the "trap door" that can be pulled shut when the animal withdraws into its house. Secondly, though it lives many miles out at sea, it cannot swim. It is one of the so-called *pelagic*, or floating, mollusks. It cements air bubbles to its foot, and by means of this self-made raft floats on the surface of the ocean.

Which deep-sea shellfish cannot swim?

Violet shells float in great numbers in the Gulf Stream and along the Atlantic Coast. When great numbers of them are washed ashore they are able to stain large beaches purple with a secretion they discharge when irritated. The violet shell attaches its eggs to the underside of its "raft" and drifts along until the eggs develop into young shellfish.

The deep-sea violet shell floats by on its bubble raft.

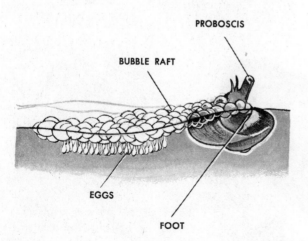

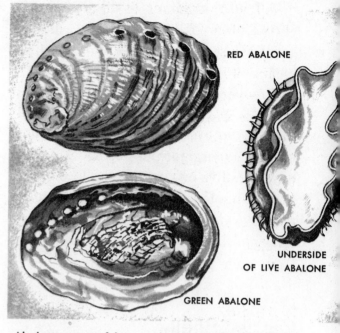

RED ABALONE

UNDERSIDE OF LIVE ABALONE

GREEN ABALONE

Abalones are useful to man both as food and jewelry.

Abalones

The *abalone*, the largest and most colorful of all Pacific Coast shells, is one of the most useful to man. Huge shell mounds found along the Pacific Coast is testimony that the early Indians relished them as food. The Indians also made bracelets and other decorative objects from abalone shells and adorned knives and other utensils with the rainbow-hued shell. Today the abalone is still a commercial food item, and one may buy canned steaks made from the large muscular foot of the animal.

In what way is the abalone used by man?

Its shell, which measures 4 to 12 inches in length, has a dull, rough surface, but a smooth, shiny inside. The thick inner layer is a rainbow-colored mother-of-pearl from which jewelry, buttons and many other ornaments are manufactured.

A feature common to all abalones is a row of holes along the side of the shell. Since the abalone breathes by means of gills — which means it must take water into its shell along with air — holes through which excess water is expelled are needed. The *red abalone,* which is 10 to 12 inches in length, has four holes; the *green abalone,* which is about 7 inches long, has six holes. The number of openings varies in different species.

Limpets

Limpets are a large family of univalves whose shells look like miniature volcanoes or Chinese hats, which they are often called. The many species vary in size from ¾ of an inch to 4 inches. Most of them have a conical, somewhat depressed shell, and a number of species have a hole in the peak of the spiral. Limpets generally prefer the cooler waters of the oceans, though many varieties may be collected at low tide on the Atlantic and Pacific shores.

Why are limpets often called Chinese hats?

A limpet grows attached to rocks by means of its broad foot, and since the animal has no operculum, it protects itself by pulling the shell tightly over its body. The foot acts like a suction cup. Its pull is so strong that it would be difficult to pull the limpet loose from its anchorage without breaking the shell. However, by making use of the moments when the limpet lifts itself a little in order to breathe, it is possible to pry it loose by slipping the blade of a knife between the foot and the rock. Some species attach themselves to algae or seaweed. Limpets feed on plants that grow on rocks, scraping the food off with their rasplike tongues which may be twice as long as the animal. Most species are grayish brown in color, thus blending with the rocks to which they cling.

The largest limpet in American waters is the *great keyhole limpet* of the Pacific. It may grow to a length of 4 inches. *Lister's keyhole limpet,* no larger than 2 inches, occurs from Florida to British Guiana and is often called the *volcano shell.* Two other interesting species are the *rough limpet,* a little over 1 inch in size, and without a hole in its top; and the *tortoise shell limpet,* a cold-water mollusk about 1 inch in length, found from Labrador to Connecticut. The latter's shell is bluish white with brown markings — giving it its name — and is sometimes called the *Atlantic plate limpet.*

ANTILLEAN LIMPET

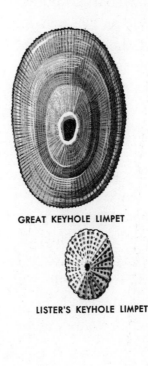

GREAT KEYHOLE LIMPET

LISTER'S KEYHOLE LIMPET

LIMPETS ON ROCK

Periwinkles

Periwinkles are a large family of uni-valves with sturdy shells having few whorls, and range in color from a grayish white on olive brown to purple; some are spotted. Periwinkles were introduced from Europe — where they are a favored seafood — to American waters about a hundred years ago, and today they are among the most abundant shells on the Atlantic seacoast. Periwinkles, which are ½ to 1 inch in length, are the oysterman's friends because they feed mainly on seaweed, and thereby prevent an overgrowth of weeds that might smother oysters.

Why is the periwinkle man's friend?

As a group, they are not particularly bright in color. The *common periwinkle* is brownish olive to black. The glossy shell of the *smooth periwinkle* is yellow or orange. The *zebra periwinkle* is whitish with wavy dark-brown stripes. The *rough periwinkle* has a coarse, yellowish-gray shell with four or five convex whorls. Strangely, its shell is smooth, with yellow and black spots, when the animal is young.

Whelks

There are many species of *whelks,* which vary in color, shape and size — some are tiny and others have shells as large as 15 inches. One of the largest is the *lightning whelk,* or *left-handed whelk.* It has a grayish-white shell with purple streaks, and spirals which twist to the left. It is found in waters from South Carolina to Florida.

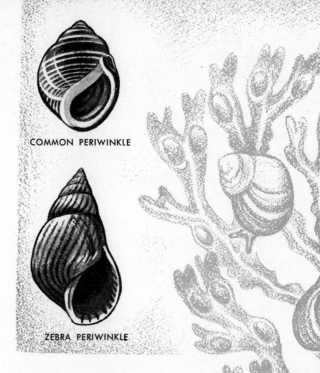

COMMON PERIWINKLE

ZEBRA PERIWINKLE

From Cape Cod, Massachusetts, to central Florida, occurs the *knobbed whelk,* whose shell is yellowish gray with an orange-red interior. It gets its name from the blunt nodes grown on the shell at each stage of the univalve's development. It is edible and a good fish bait. Other species found on American coasts are the *tabled Neptune,* the *ten-ridge whelk* and the *pear whelk.*

In the summer, strings of egg-cases of the knobbed and the *channeled whelk* can be found on beaches. The female digs a hole in the sand and anchors her first eggs to a pebble. Then she secretes a fluid that forms a tough casing around all of them. To this casing she joins a second one, and continues the process until she has made a long string amounting to dozens of egg-cases. Each one contains as many as twenty eggs, and all are held together by means of a tough cord. The female can make ten to fifteen egg-cases, or as many as 300

How do whelks make egg-cases?

QUEEN CONCH

FIGHTING CONCH

LIGHTNING WHELK

TABLED NEPTUNE

EMPEROR HELMET

CHANNELED WHELK AND EGGS

eggs in a single day. After a few weeks, the cases will contain tiny whelk shells, each about 1/16 to ¼ of an inch long.

Whelks feed on oysters, drilling holes in the oysters' shells, much as the oyster drill does, but whelks are also scavengers of the sea.

Conch Shells

A widespread carnivorous group of univalves are the *conch shells*. Practically all species of these warmwater shells are thick, with enlarged body whorls, and a thickened and expanded outer lip. The operculum is formed like a claw and does not close completely. The conch has an awkward but effective way of moving. It hooks the clawlike operculum in the sand, raises its shell high in the air, and topples over.

How does the conch walk?

The adult *queen conch* is between 8 and 12 inches in length, and its shell is yellowish on the outside and rose-pink on the inside. It has, for a long time, been a popular article in homes and souvenir shops. Another interesting species is the *fighting conch* of the West Indies and southern Florida, whose shell grows 3 to 5 inches long. It is deep yellowish brown on the outside and deep orange or purple on the inside.

Helmet Shells

Helmet shells are shaped like stubby cones with very thick lips, and are characteristically similar to the conches to which they are related. Because the shell is very thick and composed of layers of material in contrasting colors, helmets are widely used in the manufacture of cameos. Actually, most shells would fit these requirements, but only the helmets are thick enough to be carved easily without damage.

Why are helmet shells used for making cameos?

The most colorful of the species are

29

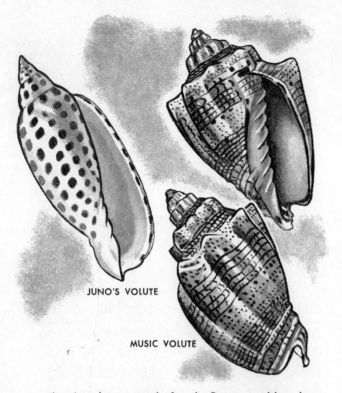

JUNO'S VOLUTE

MUSIC VOLUTE

Juno's volute, named after the Roman goddess Juno, and the *music volute* are both members of the family of vase shells. *Volute* is a word meaning "to roll."

the *king helmet* — 4 to 9 inches in size; the *emperor helmet* — slightly larger than the king; and the *flame helmet* — 3 to 5 inches in length.

Juno's Volute

If you are a stamp collector, you know

Why did the Juno's volute cost $100?

that it is unusual rarity that makes a stamp a wanted item. In shell collecting, it is both rarity and beauty that make a shell a

collector's item. The *Juno's volute* is a shell that once sold for about a hundred dollars because it was both extremely hard to find and beautiful. Today, it can be bought for as little as two or three dollars. It is still a beautiful specimen, of course, but it is no longer rare since fishermen found large beds of these shells in the waters off the coast of Yucatan, Mexico.

The Juno's volute is 4 to 5 inches long. It is pinkish white with rows of reddish spots, and has four or five whorls among which is a large body whorl. The outer surface of the shell is smooth. This mollusk lives between rocks and coral in deep water from South Carolina to the Gulf of Mexico. Good specimens are seldom washed up on shore.

Wentletrap

Another once-very rare shell is the

What does "wentletrap" mean?

precious wentletrap. Wentletrap is a Dutch word meaning "winding staircase" and for this reason, the various species are also called *staircase shells.* The precious wentletrap of the China coast can be bought today from dealers for about five or ten dollars or even less. Once it

GROWTH OF LIP OF WENTLETRAP

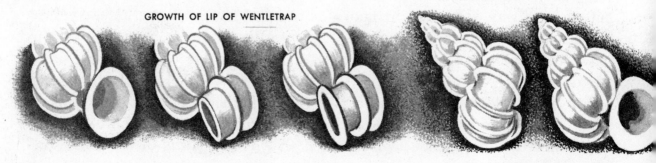

PRECIOUS WENTLETRAP

was so rare that collectors were willing to pay very large sums for a specimen.

Species of wentletraps occur in virtually all seas. The shells, usually white and polished, average 1½ inches in length — the exact length varies with the particular species. They are high-spired with many rounded whorls gradually decreasing in size. The ridges at the ends of the whorls are formed by a thickening of the outer lip of the shell. Even the common wentletraps are delicately and gracefully built, and include the *lined wentletrap*, the *crowded wentletrap*, the *little staircase* and the *ladder shell*.

Cone Shells

The members of the large *cone shell* family are, as the name suggests, cone-shaped. Each cone has many whorls at its top, and the lip is almost the length of the shell. Most species are found among the coral reefs in tropical seas, and some which live in the Indian and South Pacific oceans are capable of producing a poison from a gland within their bodies. The poison goes through ducts in the tiny teeth at the end of the mollusk's tongue and may be injected into shellfish with which

How do they inject poison?

they come in contact. Persons stung by these cones may become very ill.

Only a few species of cones are found in American waters — from the Carolinas to Florida — and these are harmless. They include the *alphabet cone* that has a 3-inch-long shell, a creamy white color, and spiral rows of orange or brown dots that often resemble the letters of the Chinese alphabet; the *Florida cone* that averages 1½ inches in length, and is yellowish with yellow-brown markings; and the *mouse cone* that is only 1 inch long, yellow in color with reddish spots. It often has a light-colored central band with faint spiral lines. All species are carnivorous.

Which cone has Chinese letters?

An extremely rare species is the *glory-of-the-seas cone* from the waters of the East Indies and it is perhaps the most valuable of all shells. (An illustration of it appears on page 33.)

Tulip Shells

The largest univalves in American waters belong to the *band shell* or *tulip shell* family. These shells are thick, spired and sharply pointed. The *true tulip shell* and the *banded tulip shell*

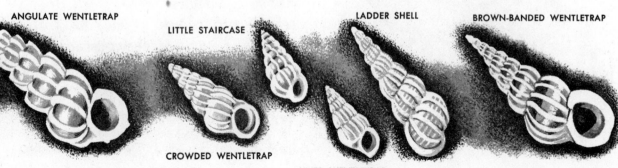

ANGULATE WENTLETRAP

LITTLE STAIRCASE

CROWDED WENTLETRAP

LINED WENTLETRAP

LADDER SHELL

BROWN-BANDED WENTLETRAP

range from 3 to 6 inches in length, and are pink in color with bands of dark brown and streaks of red.

The *giant band shell,* or *Florida horse conch,* ranges from 1 to 2 feet in length.

Which is the largest American univalve?

Its outer color is brown with dark brown spiral lines, while the inside of the shell is orange-red. The animal itself is brick red. This largest of all American univalves can be found in waters from North Carolina to Brazil. It uses its very large foot and great weight to smother and crush its prey.

Olive Shells

Olive shells are smooth, glossy and sometimes brightly colored. They are 1½ to 2½ inches long and are found

When is the best time to find an olive?

in warm seas. Olives bury themselves in the sand in shallow waters and poke their siphons up into the clear water near the surface. In this position they are hard to find, but olives come out of the sand at night, and at low tide they may be easily found.

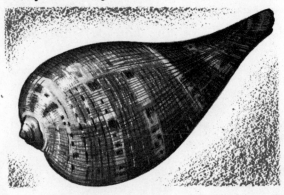

Moon Shells

Species of *moon shells* are found on the

How do moon shells prey on shellfish?

mud and sand flats of most Atlantic and Pacific shores. They are sometimes called *natica shells* because of their family name, *Naticidae.* The shells are globular and usually have greater width than length. Some species have button-like tops which have resulted in popular names such as *shark eye, bull's eye* and *cat's eye.* All moon shells are carnivorous and feed on other sea life which they overwhelm and smother with an especially large foot. When extended, this foot often conceals an entire shellfish. Moon shells produce a glue from their bodies with which they cement sand grains to build a protective ring for their eggs.

The *spotted moon shell* has a delicate

What do "cats" and "sharks" look like?

coloring—pale bluish white with chestnut-brown spiral bars and spots. It is about 1½ inches long. The cat's eye and shark eye species are about 1 to 2½ inches long. The "cat" is colored rich brown on the outside and pure brown inside. The outside of the "shark" is blue-white and brown on the top. The *common Northern moon shell,* found from New Jersey to Maine, the *Northern natica,* found off the coasts of Newfoundland and Nova Scotia, and the

The *common fig shell,* which is related to the tropical tun, or cask shells, is three to four inches in length. The body, when protruding from the shell, is bigger.

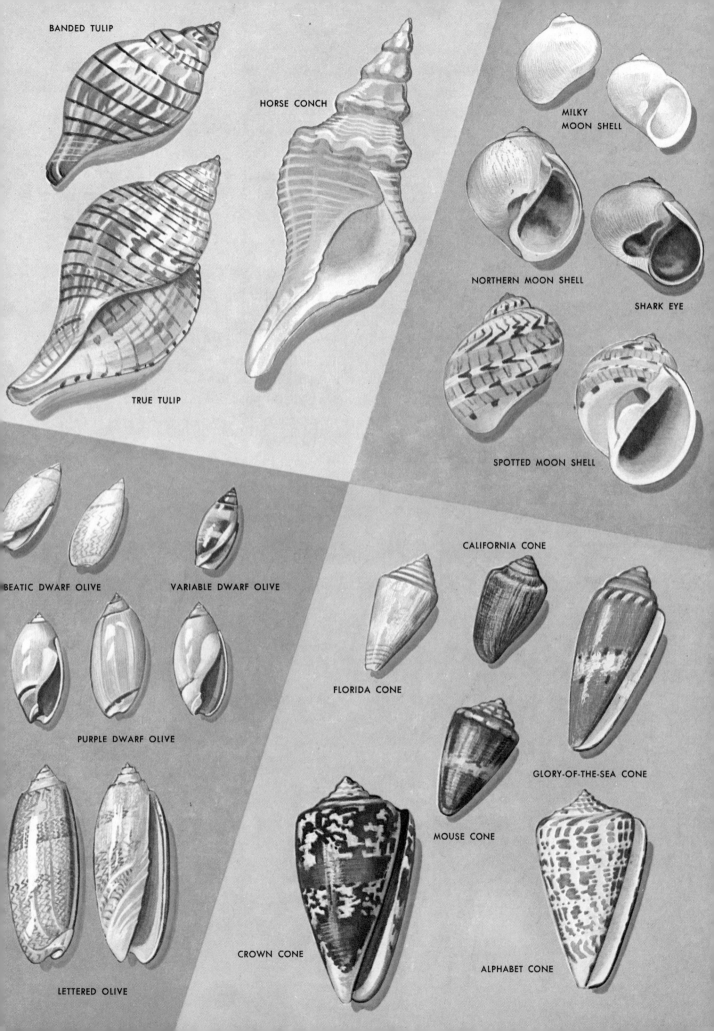

BANDED TULIP

HORSE CONCH

MILKY MOON SHELL

NORTHERN MOON SHELL

SHARK EYE

TRUE TULIP

SPOTTED MOON SHELL

BEATIC DWARF OLIVE

VARIABLE DWARF OLIVE

CALIFORNIA CONE

FLORIDA CONE

PURPLE DWARF OLIVE

GLORY-OF-THE-SEA CONE

MOUSE CONE

CROWN CONE

ALPHABET CONE

LETTERED OLIVE

milky moon shell, found on beaches from Florida to Texas, are a few of the many other moon species.

Other Univalves

A few other univalves of interest include the *top shell* and the *turban shell,* both of which derive a name from their shapes; the *slipper,* or *boat shell,* which has a little platform similar to the decks of old sailing ships; and the beautifully colored ½-inch-long *bubble shell,* whose shell house is smaller than the animal which lives within it. (See illustrations on pages 36-37.)

Chitons

Chitons, another class of mollusks, are the most primitive of the phylum *Mollusca.* There are so many varieties of chitons that if they did not all have the same basic

What feature is common to all chitons?

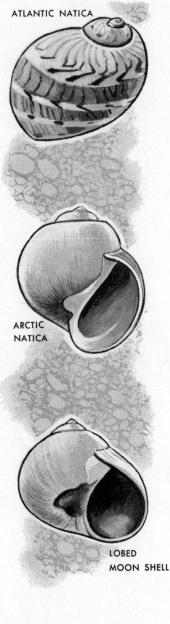

ATLANTIC NATICA

ARCTIC NATICA

LOBED MOON SHELL

The body is shown protruding from the moon shell (below). It makes a sand "ring" (right) in which eggs are placed.

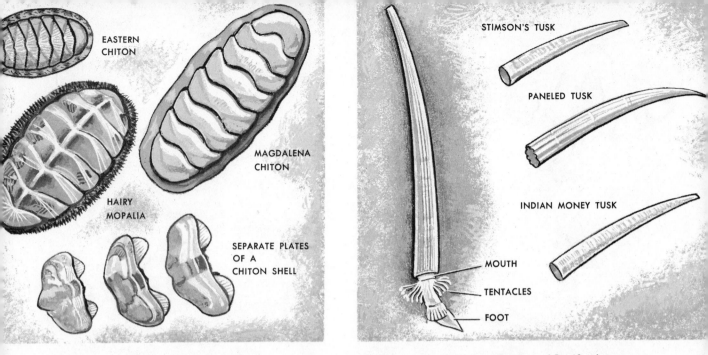

EASTERN CHITON

MAGDALENA CHITON

HAIRY MOPALIA

SEPARATE PLATES OF A CHITON SHELL

STIMSON'S TUSK

PANELED TUSK

INDIAN MONEY TUSK

MOUTH

TENTACLES

FOOT

Chitons and tusk shells represent two separate classes of mollusks common to both the Atlantic and Pacific shores.

structure, it would be difficult to believe that all belonged to the same class. They range in size from ⅓ of an inch to more than 10 inches — and in color, from blue-green to dull brown. The one physical characteristic common to all is a shell made up of eight plates, overlapping like the shingles of a roof, and held together with a girdle along the outer edge. Beneath the shell is a mantle that completely covers the body of the animal. It has a mouth and a tongue in an otherwise poorly developed head. There is also a digestive tract, a pair of kidneys, a primitive nervous system, a heart that pumps colorless blood and a very flattened foot. They are plant-eaters and feed on seaweed.

How do they look like armor and cradles? Chitons are more common along the Pacific than the Atlantic Coast, and since they prefer darkness, will usually attach themselves to the underside of rocks. Chitons are also called *coat-of-mail shells*, because their shells resemble the armor worn by knights of the Middle Ages. They are also known as *sea cradles,* for when disturbed they curl up in the likeness of a cradle. To loosen a chiton from a rock — usually rocks which are exposed on the beach at low tide — a knife blade slipped under its foot will serve the purpose.

The *common Eastern chiton*, which is less than 1 inch long, the *hairy mopalia*, about 1½ inches in length, and the *Magdalena chiton*, 2 to 3 inches long, are just three of the many species found in American waters.

Tusk Shells

How do tusk shells stand on their heads? *Tusk shells*, which are rarely more than 2 inches long, represent another class of mollusks. Characterizing them is a slightly curved, tubular shell that is open at both ends. With its clamlike

HAIRY TRITON

APPLE MUREX

CHESTNUT COWRY

PEAR WHELK

YELLOW COWRY

GREEN ABALONE

EMARGINATE DOGWINKLE

HELMET SHELL

ANGULAR TRITON

ATLANTIC PLATE LIMPET

ATLANTIC DOGWINKLE

RIBBED TOP SHELL

BAIRD'S SPINY MARGARITE

JUJUBE TOP SHELL

GREAT TOP SHELL

CHANNELED TOP SHEL

TAPESTRY TURBAN

CARPENTER'S DWARF TUR

SMOOTH ATLANTIC TEGULA

BLACK TEGULA

GOLD-MOUTHED TURBAN

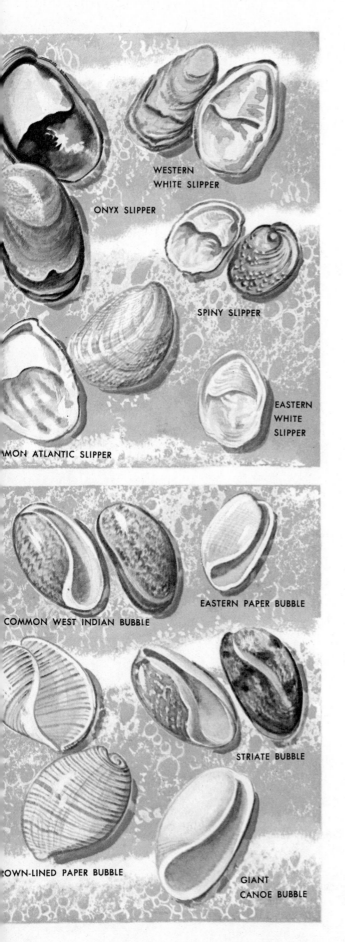

WESTERN WHITE SLIPPER

ONYX SLIPPER

SPINY SLIPPER

EASTERN WHITE SLIPPER

MON ATLANTIC SLIPPER

COMMON WEST INDIAN BUBBLE

EASTERN PAPER BUBBLE

STRIATE BUBBLE

OWN-LINED PAPER BUBBLE

GIANT CANOE BUBBLE

foot, this little mollusk digs into sand or mud, resting there with only the pointlike end of the tube sticking up out of the water. And since the animal's head rests directly on its foot, it may be said, in a manner of speaking, that the tusk shell stands on its head.

This mollusk's radula, the tongue-like organ, has several rows of teeth, and around its mouth are several stringy filaments that wave rapidly back and forth. This action pulls into the shell the tiny creatures on which the tusk feeds. Tusk shells, also called *tooth shells,* are usually smooth, but a few species, such as the *paneled tusk,* have ribs running down the length of the tube. Some species are greenish in color, others are brown, but most are ivory white.

How does the tusk shell feed?

The Pacific Coast Indians used to string tusk shells into necklaces and also used them as money. The Western Plains Indians employed them as ornaments for clothing. More than one hundred species are found on American coasts, and among them are *Stimson's tusk,* which is 1 to 2 inches long, the *Indian money tuck,* about 2 inches in length, and the *ivory tusk,* 1 to 2½ inches long.

Cephalopoda

Cephalopods are the "head-footed" mollusks. In this class are the *squid, cuttlefish, octopus* and *nautilus.* Of these, only the nautilus has an outside shell. The squid has a thin, flat plate of horny shell-like material within its body called a *pen*. The cuttlefish has a broader plate, also internal, known as *cuttlebone,* which is often placed in bird cages as a salt stick. The octopus has no shell.

Squid, Cuttlefish, Octopus

The foot of these related cephalopod mollusks has de-

How many arms do they have?

veloped into a head from which branch a number of arms, or *tentacles,* surrounding the mouth. The squid and cuttlefish each have ten tentacles, two of which are longer than the others, but the octopus has only eight arms. Each sea animal's tentacles are equipped with rows of suction cups, or disks, that are used to grasp and hold the prey upon which they feed. Each has a coarse, rasping tongue, a horny beak and two powerful jaws with which to tear apart prey swept into their mouths by the snake-like tentacles. All have highly developed eyes.

They move by drawing water into a

How are they like jet planes?

mantle cavity of the body and forcibly squeezing it out again through a funnel, or *siphon*. This action propels the squid and octopus backward, and the cuttlefish forward or backward, in a form of jet propulsion. Although the octopus is capable of propelling itself in jet fashion, it usually prefers to move slowly near rocks in shallow sea bottoms.

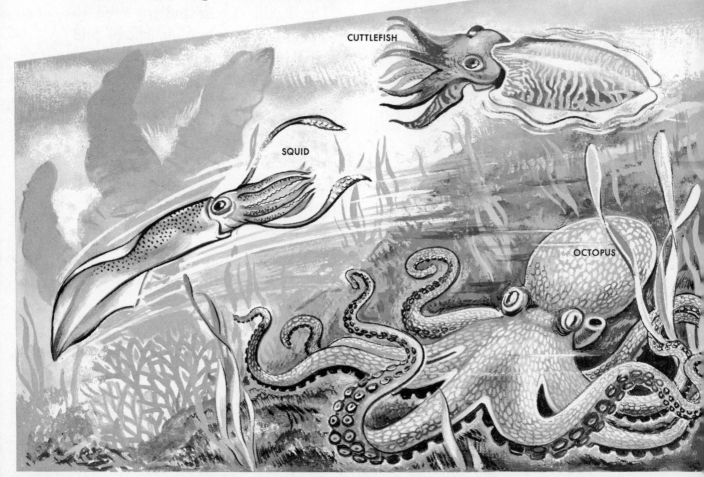

CUTTLEFISH

SQUID

OCTOPUS

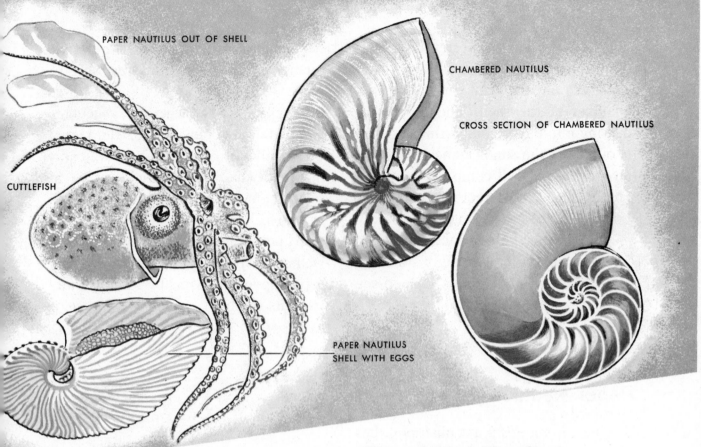

PAPER NAUTILUS OUT OF SHELL

CUTTLEFISH

CHAMBERED NAUTILUS

CROSS SECTION OF CHAMBERED NAUTILUS

PAPER NAUTILUS
SHELL WITH EGGS

Chambered Nautilus

These cephalopods have glands from which they can, **How do they escape enemies?** when attacked by an enemy, expel a dark fluid. This inky fluid forms a dense cloud behind which the creature can hide or escape. The squid and octopus can also change color quickly and this fairly well matches certain sea backgrounds as an added protection.

Squids vary in size from a few inches to the 50-foot *giant squid*. Cuttlefish vary in length, and range from a few inches to about 6 feet. Octopuses measure — end to end of outstretched tentacles — from a few inches to the 20-foot *giant octopus* of the Pacific Ocean.

The young of these cephalopods are hatched from eggs that are laid in clusters on rocks, and look like miniature adults when they are born.

The *chambered nautilus* has a spiral shell not unlike certain univalves, **Why is it called "chambered"?** though the animal within is a cephalopod. The shell is yellowish white with reddish-brown spiral bands and has a very large dark spot at its center. The inside is beautifully lined with mother-of-pearl and is divided into a number of neatly separated chambers which give the mollusk its name.

When this cephalopod is young, its shell has only one small chamber. **How does it build its house?** But as the mollusk grows it inches forward because of the need for more space to accommodate its increasing size. When the nautilus is settled in the new chamber, it builds a wall behind itself from the secretions of its mantle. Thus, the animal always makes its home in the last, or outermost, chamber of the shell. The process of moving into larger compartments when it outgrows the smaller ones results in an interesting shell composed of many "rooms," each one representing a distinct phase of the nautilus' development. The sealed-off chambers are filled with air and are watertight, thereby enabling the nautilus — a deep-sea dweller — to float.

her uppermost tentacles. The fragile quality of this shell has given it the name "paper" nautilus. She deposits her eggs in the shell where they incubate and hatch. People used to think that the nautilus floated along on water by making two of its tentacles serve as sails. It doesn't, but for this reason, it is also called the *Argonaut,* after the ship and sailors of Greek mythology, as well as the *paper sailor*. But, like other cephalopods, it swims by forcing water from its siphon.

Paper Nautilus

The *paper nautilus* is a cephalopod that

Why did people think of it as a sailor?

has eight tentacles. The female of the species, which is much larger than the male nautilus, secretes a very fragile and papery shell case from two of

An empty moon shell makes a perfect home for the hermit crab, a crab which seeks shell "houses."

Shell Collecting

Certainly many of you have taken home

Where can you find shells?

from a visit to the beach a shell that you displayed for a time on a bookshelf, a desk or a table. Perhaps you even brought home a whole bucketful of shells. But now, having learned a good deal of information about these colorful specimens of the sea, you might want to start a collection. You don't have to be at the

seashore to begin one, because many shells can be found in lakes, streams, ponds, swamps, tidal pools and sandy flats. You might even dig up a fossil shell in your own back yard. No one — not even the museums — has collected specimens of every kind. In fact, several new specimens are discovered each year. Just imagine the thrill if you were to discover a new shell, or even a very rare one!

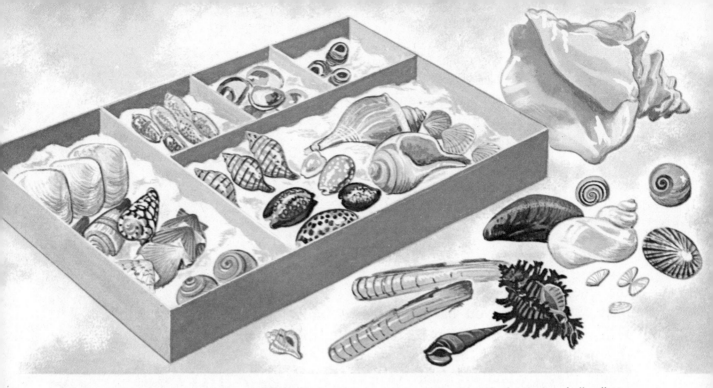

A display case with separate compartments in which to keep specimens is useful to the beginning shell collector.

At first, as other beginners do, you may collect whatever you can find — even discolored and broken shells — that can be replaced later with better specimens. Still later, you may wish to collect specimens of only one or two families. You will meet other collectors, especially if your friends also become interested in this hobby, and trade "doubles" with them just as stamp collectors do. You might buy one or two shells that are missing from your collection and which would be hard to get otherwise. As your collection grows, you will become more selective, and in a surprisingly short time, find that you have collected a rather large number of interesting and possibly valuable shells.

But however you start your collection, you will find that much of the fun is in going out to hunt for the shells yourself.

Most of the shells you find along the beaches are "dead" shells. This means that not only has the animal died, but the sun has faded the colors and waves have blunted or broken the shell's edge or dulled the polish by rolling it in the sand. However, some of these are not too beach-worn and may be placed in the collection of the beginner. They can always be replaced afterward.

What are "dead" shells?

The next better-quality shell is one which contains a mollusk that has recently died. Such shells will be tossed up on the beach by the waves, especially after a storm, or left on the beach at low tide. After a storm, you may find shells along the shore that usually live only in deep seas. Become familiar with weather conditions and learn the hours of high and low tides in your area.

How does knowledge of weather help?

Usually local newspapers or radio and television stations give this information in their weather forecasts.

Having started your collection with

"dead" shells and "recently dead" ones, you can move on to the best specimens — the ones taken when the mollusk is alive. To do this, you have to know something about the living habits of the mollusks whose shells you want. Knowing where and when and what to look for is a step that will come with increased knowledge and experience. If you are an excellent swimmer and diver, you can reach certain shells that live in deeper waters. Or you can make a dredge and drag it over the sea bottom. But you should not hunt for shells in deep waters unless you are accompanied by one or more adults who are also excellent swimmers. The presence of a small boat, such as a rowboat, is especially recommended on such field trips, not only because it is an important safety factor, but also because you will need a place to store your equipment. Those of you who know how to skin-dive with aqualungs have an added advantage.

To begin your shell collecting, you will need the following articles of equipment: an old pair of dungarees, or swimming trunks if you plan to go deeper; a pair of sneakers or old tennis shoes; a bag or basket made of waterproof material; a few small jars or plastic containers or bottles for the smaller specimens; an old toothbrush to clean some shells on the spot; a pair of heavy cotton gloves; a pocket knife; a small shovel; a notebook; and a pencil. If you can carry still more, an enamel bucket is helpful.

While most of your shells can be placed safely in a bag or basket, some species of mollusks contract a great deal when taken from the water, with the result that their shells sometimes break. Therefore, it is well to put them in a pail of water as soon as they are found. Do not mix large and small shells together, because many of the smaller ones are fragile and may be chipped by the weight of the larger specimens. Experienced shell collectors will also want a complete field guide of sea shells with detailed and specialized information, which is useful in identifying various species.

Where are the best shells found?

What equipment will you need?

To get the best shells, you must "bring 'em back alive," and you will have to clean them. Very small shells can be put in a shady place and allowed to dry. In a short time, the odor will disappear, and if the shell is a gastropod, the operculum will stay in place. Use this same method for bivalves only if you want to display them closed. But if you want to display two-shelled specimens with the valves open, like butterfly wings, put them in fresh water. This will make them open, and you can then easily remove the animal with a small knife. By putting a drop of glycerin on the ligament that holds the two shells together, it will not dry up, and the two valves will not break apart.

How do you clean your shell "catch"?

A univalve that is fairly small can also be placed in pure grain alcohol, or in a 4% solution of formaldehyde, both of which are available at your local drugstore. Leave the shell in the solution for a few days and then allow it to dry in the shade. It will be odorless when dry, but frequently the operculum will have disappeared, having been pulled into the shell by the contraction of the mollusk's body.

How do you remove a mollusk from its shell?

You must remove the body entirely from large univalves. To do this, boil the mollusk. Never drop the specimen directly into boiling water, however, because this may crack the shell or fog its polished surface. Put the shell in lukewarm water and bring it slowly to a boil. How long you keep it in the boiling water will depend on the size and structure of the shell—usually the time varies from a few minutes to a half-hour. Remove the shell after the water has cooled. Then, using a stiff piece of wire that has a hook at one end — or a crocheting needle — insert it in the canal end of the shell, push in as far as possible, and give the wire a circular twist to roll the animal out. Be careful not to press on the lip too hard. Some shells break easily. If it doesn't come out, repeat the boiling process.

You must start to remove the mollusk's body as soon as the shell is cool. If you allow it to get too cold, the animal shrinks far up into the shell, and removing it becomes more difficult. For this reason, do not boil too many shells at the same time.

As soon as the mollusk is removed, cut the operculum from the body with a knife and allow the shell to dry. If it has lost its polish, rub it with mineral oil. Glue the operculum to some absorbent cotton or to a pipe cleaner, then put it back in its original position in the shell.

After all this is done, most specimens need no additional cleaning, but some may still have a growth on the outside of their shells. Usually, the growth can be removed by brushing with a toothbrush and soapy water. If this doesn't work, you may have to add about two teaspoons of laundry bleach. However, there is a disadvantage in this method, because the bleach may fade the shell's colors or dull its finish.

How do you remove a growth from a shell?

A collector's fun is not only in finding the shells, but also in sorting, labeling and displaying them. Some collectors sort shells according to size and color, some group them by the regions in which they are found, and some separate them according to the five classes of mollusks. The last method is more scientific and offers greater educational rewards for the beginning collector. Use a large box for each class, subdividing the box into compartments for the individual species that belong to the class.

How should you sort shells?

You may want to add the size of the shells to your catalogue entry and this can be done by using a caliper, an instrument that has a pair of curved legs which are fastened to each other by a screw. By placing the two ends of the caliper on the shell at both its widest and longest dimensions, and then using a ruler to measure the distance between these points, you can determine both the width and length of the specimen. References to the size of shells in most sources, as well as in this book, are usually measurements of the length — from the tip of the apex, or point, down to the lip, or bottom.

How can you measure shells?

Calipers are inexpensive and usually may be purchased at hardware stores and five-and-dime shops. A more precise instrument is the caliper rule. Because it has a fixed rule and a sliding jaw, measurements can be taken instantly without the added use of a straight ruler.

Scientists say that the value of a collection depends greatly on the way it is labeled and catalogued. Paste a numbered sticker on the shell, or put the number directly on the shell with India ink. Then write the same number in a notebook, and alongside it the name of the shell. For now, it will be sufficient to write only the *popular* name of the shell. However, leave room to write the *scientific* name, which you can learn from a field guide book. Then add as many details as you can — the date and time of day

How should you label shells?

when you found the shell, exactly where you found it, and whether it was dead or alive, weather conditions of the previous day, and any other information that you think may be of value.

The scientific name usually has two parts. The first is the genus, or *generic* name, such as *Tellina* (meaning "Tellin"). The second part is the species, or *specific* name, such as *lineata* (which is popularly called "rose petal"). Frequently, there is a third part—the name of the person who discovered and first described the shell. Perhaps one

day your own name will become part of the scientific name of a shell.

Here is an example of how an entry in your notebook might look:

no. 16
Measled Cowry
Cypraea zebra Linne
Found Sept. 12, 1960, at 7. a. m.
on the beach at Key West, Florida
Animal dead when found
High winds the day before.

Some Things to Make With Shells

Obtain an olive shell about 2½ inches long, a mussel about 4 inches long, and a winkle about ½ inch long. Hold two 5-inch

How can you make a butterfly from olive and mussel shells?

pieces of pipe cleaner parallel and with their ends even. Insert them into the lip of the olive shell as far as they will go, and affix them firmly with adhesive cement. Separate the mussel's two valves. Drill a hole — into which the pipe cleaner will just fit — at the hinge

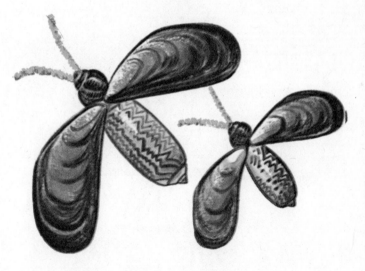

of each valve. Insert the pipe cleaners into the mussel valves in the manner shown in the illustration. Secure the pipe cleaners to the insides of the valves with a generous supply of cement.

Using a large dab of cement, affix the winkle to the olive shell just where the wings (the mussel valves) meet. When all the cement has dried, bend

45

two paper clips into the shape of antennas and paste them to the head. Your butterfly will look even better if you paint its wings and body.

How can you make a doll from scallops? You will need nine scallops of about the same size and color, a doll face, some pipe cleaners and adhesive cement. Cover the outside of a small teacup with wax paper. Using the cup as a base, cement four shells together, as shown in the illustration, to make the doll's skirt. Cement a layer of absorbent cotton at the points where the shells join in order to make them hold better. Let the cement dry.

Cut a seven-inch piece of pipe cleaner. Fold it in half. Bend the doubled end so that it fits into the hinge-end of the scallop that is to be the hat. Cement the pipe cleaner inside the hat-shell, and then cement the doll face to the pipe cleaner. Use a five-inch pipe cleaner for the doll's arms. Cement it to the first one, so that when the body-shell is put in place, the ends of the pipe cleaner will stick out on both sides as arms.

Use two scallops for the body. Place them so that the hinge on each is just below the hinge of the shell that forms the head. Thus, the hinges of the two shells will be together, one in front and one in back, surrounding the first pipe cleaner, with their concave sides together. Cement these shells together at their edges. Hold them in place with some rubber bands while the cement is drying.

Lastly, cement two more scallops on the skirt. Poke the body pipe cleaner (the first one) between the hinges at the top of the skirt, and cement the pipe cleaner in place. When the cement is dry, tie a ribbon bow around the doll's neck to hide the pipe cleaner. Make a small bouquet out of cellophane and paste it in place. Decorate the skirt and hat with paint.

Scallops make decorative ash trays. An unfinished piece of driftwood serves as a stand.

Obtain a scallop shell that is more than 2½ inches wide,

How can you make an ash tray out of scallops?

and two small scallops about ¾ of an inch wide. Glue or cement the two small shells to the outside of the large one, as in the illustration. Wipe off the surplus cement and allow the rest to set firmly. If you have obtained a really large scallop for your tray, you can then cement two small shells of almost any kind to the "shoulders" at the hinged part of the big shell. Put these two shells on the opposite side of the first two. The first two shells serve as legs to steady the ash tray; the second two shells serve as decoration.

You will need a large cowry, such as the tropical tiger cowry, 2½ to 3 inches long; a very small cowry, less than ½ inch long; four cockle shells, about ½ inch in diameter; and a small wentletrap, or other pointed shell. Turn the large cowry so that its lip is uppermost. Put a large dab of adhesive cement on each of the four corners of the shell. Place the convex side of a cockle into each dab of cement. The cockles form the feet of the turtle. Attach these shells evenly, so that the finished turtle will stand steadily.

How can you make a turtle out of shells?

When the cement on the feet has dried, attach the small cowry to the

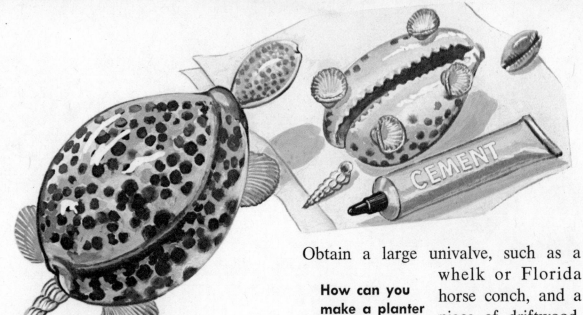

pointed end of the large cowry, again using a large dab of cement. The lips of both cowries should face in the same direction.

When the head is firmly fixed, attach the wentletrap as a tail, employing the same method used for the head and feet. When all the cement is dry, turn the lips of the cowries downward, and the turtle will stand on its feet.

How can you make a planter out of a large univalve? Obtain a large univalve, such as a whelk or Florida horse conch, and a piece of driftwood. If necessary, clean the driftwood with a steel brush, sandpaper, or steel wool. With a knife, cut a depression in the wood, so that the rounded side of the shell fits into it. Cover the bottom of this depression with adhesive cement and put the shell firmly into the cement. When the cement dries, you will have a planter. You might decorate the planter by pasting a few small shells of different colors on it.